# The Ultimate Sports Fans' Cookbook

## Festive Recipes for Inside the Home and Outside the Stadium

By David Bowers

Skyhorse Publishing

All Rights Reserved. No part of this book may be reproduced in any man-
ner without the express written consent of the publisher, except in the
case of brief excerpts in critical reviews or articles. All inquiries should
be addressed to Skyhorse Publishing, 307 West 36th Street, 11th Floor,
New York, NY 10018.

Skyhorse Publishing books may be purchased in bulk at special dis-
counts for sales promotion, corporate gifts, fund-raising, or educational
purposes. Special editions can also be created to specifications. For
details, contact the Special Sales Department, Skyhorse Publishing, 307
West 36th Street, 11th Floor, New York, NY 10018 or info@skyhorsepub-
lishing.com.

Skyhorse® and Skyhorse Publishing® are registered trademarks of
Skyhorse Publishing, Inc.®, a Delaware corporation.

Visit our website at www.skyhorsepublishing.com.

10 9 8 7 6 5 4 3 2 1

Library of Congress Cataloging-in-Publication Data is available on file.

ISBN: 978-1-62636-407-3

Printed in China

# CONTENTS

## Chapter Four: The Stanley Cup

## Chapter Five: The Super Bowl

# INTRODUCTION

GAME SEASON IS on! And it's time to invite all your friends around to watch the playoffs. Naturally, if people are coming over to watch the big game, you've got to feed them.

Finding food to feed sports fans is an ongoing challenge—any given recipe needs to make a lot, be easy on the cook, and not be drippy or messy, since excited people might be jumping up and down while eating it. Ideally, it's also extremely tasty, maybe even memorable, and preferably not too totally laden with fat.

Such a menu is really not too much to ask. With this cookbook in hand, you'll find lots of simply delicious fan-friendly foods, organized loosely by sport. So, whether you're making Hockey Puck Fudge for the Stanley Cup or Bourbon Barbecue Meatballs for the Super Bowl, you're sure to find a whole lot of crowd-pleasing fare that will have your favorite sports fans roaring for more. And with make-ahead tips and prep ideas . . . well, you might just get to watch the game yourself.

A sports party that absolutely everyone can enjoy? That's a real winner.

Key

Make and Take
to a Tailgate

Make on Site
at a Tailgate

# CHAPTER 1

# BOWL GAMES

FOOTBALL FANS COME to the table ready to get rowdy . . . and eat a lot. Cold weather means that heartiness is the name of the game during bowl season. It's a good time to turn on the oven and fill the house with fragrant foods, hearty pastas, and lots of rib-sticking snacks. And don't be shy about dessert. Just because your guests ate everything on the table before halftime doesn't mean they're totally full. A little sweetness will move your football party happily into the end zone.

## On the Menu:

Ranch Pretzel Party Mix
Crispy Spiced Chickpeas
Quick Grilled Short Ribs
Molten Butternut Squash
All-in-One Lasagna
Veggie Pizza with Fried Potato Cubes
Peanut Noodles with Chicken and Cucumber
Chicken-Coconut Curry
Pecan Toffee Bars
Mini Chocolate Lava Cakes

# Ranch Pretzel Party Mix

Addictively crunchy, tangy, and herbal, this party mix will disappear by the handful—if you have a big crowd coming, you won't be sorry if you double the recipe. For ease, however, make it in two batches, or you'll have too much stuff to fit on the baking sheets. Making a homemade ranch mix adds intense layers of flavor to the finished mix, but for ease, feel free to use one envelope of ranch dressing mix instead.

*Makes 8 to 10 servings*

1 10-ounce bag pretzel minis
3 cups crunchy corn cereal (such as Corn Chex)
2 cups mixed nuts
1/3 cup oil
1/2 cup ranch seasoning (see below)

For 1 cup of ranch seasoning, toss together:
1/2 cup buttermilk powder
1/4 cup dried parsley
1 tablespoon dried chives
2 teaspoons dried dill
2 teaspoons dried whole basil leaves
2 teaspoons dry mustard
2 teaspoons kosher salt
1 teaspoon garlic powder
1 teaspoon onion powder
1/2 teaspoon black pepper

1.   Preheat the oven to 350 degrees F. Place the pretzels, corn cereal, and nuts in a large mixing bowl and toss with the oil and ranch seasoning.
2.   Pour the mixture onto two large rimmed baking sheets and bake for 15 minutes, stirring the mixture every 5 minutes, until it's toasted and hot throughout. Cool and store in an airtight container for up to a week.

# Crispy Spiced Chickpeas

Looking for a slightly healthier snack food that's nonetheless a totally addictive nibble? Roasting chickpeas at high heat makes them into crispy finger food that's still tender and creamy inside. Chili powder makes a terrific and simple coating, but you can use any spice mix you prefer: garam masala and Cajun seasoning are good, too.

*Makes 4 servings*

1 15-ounce can chickpeas, drained
2 tablespoons olive oil
1 tablespoon chili powder
1/2 teaspoon salt
1/4 teaspoon freshly ground black pepper

1.   Preheat the oven to 350 degrees F. Pour the drained chickpeas into a medium mixing bowl and pat them dry with a paper towel to remove as much moisture as you can.

2.   Toss the chickpeas with the olive oil, chili powder, salt, and pepper. Roast for 15 to 20 minutes, shaking the pan several times, until the chickpeas are just browned and crispy outside, but not burned. Serve warm or at room temperature.

# Quick Grilled Short Ribs

People tend to think of short ribs as a food that
needs to cook for hours into falling-apart tenderness.
But on the grill, you can make super-fast and exceedingly
good short ribs in record time: six minutes. In fact, if you
overcook, they will get tough as leather! Slice the meat
thin and serve with flour tortillas with a lick of plum sauce
(available in the Asian aisle of your supermarket) and some
finely sliced scallions, and you've got Peking Duck: The
Next Generation.

*Makes 4 servings*

2 pounds beef short ribs
1/3 cup soy sauce
4 garlic cloves, minced
1/4 teaspoon red pepper flakes

To serve:
8-inch flour tortillas, warmed
Plum sauce
1 bunch scallions, thinly sliced

1.   Put the ribs, soy sauce, garlic, and red pepper flakes in
a gallon-size zipper lock bag. Seal and turn the bag to coat
the ribs well. Marinate at room temperature for one hour, or
overnight in the refrigerator.
2.   To cook, preheat a gas grill on high with the lid closed
for 10 minutes. Lay the ribs on the grill rack directly over
the flame and cook for 6 minutes, turning once. Do not
overcook or the ribs will get tough.
3.   Slice the meat as thinly as possible from each rib. To
eat, lay a flour tortilla on your plate and slick it with plum
sauce. Add meat and a generous sprinkle of scallions. Roll
and eat at once.

# Molten Butternut Squash

Got any vegetarians among your crowd? This warm and satisfying side dish is an excellent main course for anyone who's not eating meat. The secret is to turn the oven up high and don't be shy about the amount of olive oil. The result is not like the overly sweet baked squash you might know. Instead, you'll get savory molten cubes of butternut that are just slightly crisp outside but meltingly tender inside, with a delicate crust of cheese.

*Makes 6 servings*

1 large butternut squash, peeled and trimmed into 1-inch
    cubes (about 8 cups)
1/3 cup all-purpose flour
1 tablespoon chopped fresh rosemary leaves
1 teaspoon salt
Freshly ground black pepper
3 garlic cloves, minced
1/3 cup olive oil
1/2 cup grated Parmesan cheese

1.   Preheat the oven to 400 degrees F and put the oil in a 9 x 13-inch baking dish. Place the dish in the oven to preheat for at least 10 minutes.
2.   Put the flour, rosemary, salt, and pepper in a gallon-size zipper lock bag and toss the squash cubes in it. Remove the hot pan from the oven and pour the floured squash into the hot oil. Sprinkle with the garlic and use a large spoon to carefully toss the squash and garlic in the heated oil. Sprinkle with the cheese and quickly return to the oven.
3.   Bake for 40 to 45 minutes, until the squash is golden and tender when pierced with a fork. Serve hot.

# All-in-One Lasagna

Who wouldn't like to make lasagna more often? But because it's so much work, for many of us it's a once-in-awhile, special occasion dish. This streamlined version is not your typical Italian style, yet it's still full of flavor.

*Makes 8 servings*

2 tablespoons olive oil
1 pound ground pork or beef
4 garlic cloves, minced
1 large onion, chopped
1 28-ounce can crushed tomatoes
1 cup water
2 teaspoons Italian seasoning
1 15-ounce container ricotta cheese
Salt and pepper
1 9-ounce box no-boil lasagna noodles
8 ounces mozzarella cheese (about 2 cups shredded)
1/2 cup grated Parmesan

1.   Preheat the oven to 350 degrees F.

2.   In a large skillet over medium-high heat, add the olive oil and cook the ground meat until lightly browned, 5 or 6 minutes. Add the onion and garlic and continue cooking until the onion is tender, 6 to 8 more minutes. Stir in the tomatoes, water, and Italian seasoning. Bring to a boil, reduce heat, and simmer for 10 minutes. Stir in the ricotta and season to taste with salt and pepper.

3.   Spread one cup of the sauce in a 9 x 13-inch baking dish. Layer on a third of the noodles, followed by a third of the sauce. Repeat, using remaining noodles and ending with sauce. Top with mozzarella and Parmesan. Bake 30 minutes, until the lasagna is bubbling and the cheese is browned.

# Veggie Pizza with Fried Potato Cubes

To make a veggie pizza really appealing for a crowd, use a wide variety of bite-size veggies. Nobody wants pizza covered in big lumps of broccoli (even when they *like* broccoli!). Precook anything that won't bake into tenderness—chop spinach leaves and sauté in a little olive oil, for example. The surprise treat is the delectable fried potato, and the other veggies are totally up to you—broccoli, spinach, whatever you like.

Store-bought pizza dough is fine, but this whole wheat crust takes only minutes longer and tastes a hundred times better. The sauce couldn't be simpler: canned tomato sauce with oregano added, which makes for a surprisingly authentic pizza parlor taste.

*Makes 2 large pizzas, about 8 servings*

2 russet potatoes
3 tablespoons olive oil, plus more as needed
Salt and pepper
1 16-ounce bag store-bought pizza dough or 1 recipe
    whole wheat crust (below)
1 15-ounce can tomato sauce
1 1/2 teaspoons dried whole oregano leaves
Shredded mozzarella
2 to 3 cups assorted veggies: blanched broccoli florets,
    sautéed spinach leaves, halved grape tomatoes, etc.

1.   Make the Fried Potato Cubes: Peel the potatoes and dice into tiny cubes, no more than 1/2 inch. Heat the olive oil in a skillet over medium-high heat and add the potatoes. Cook, stirring occasionally, until the potatoes are golden and tender, about 10 minutes. Remove to a paper towel-lined plate and sprinkle with salt and pepper.

2.  Preheat the oven to 475 degrees F. Divide the dough in half and put each half on a baking sheet sprinkled with flour or cornmeal. Spread each half into large ovals. Spoon tomato sauce onto each pie and sprinkle each pie with half the oregano. Bake for 10 minutes.

3.  Remove the pizzas from the oven and top with cheese, potato cubes, and veggies as desired. Bake for an additional 10 to 15 minutes, until the crusts are crisp and cheese is melted. Serve at once.

## Whole Wheat Pizza Crust

*Makes 2 large crusts*

1 package active dry yeast
1 cup warm water
1 teaspoon sugar
2 tablespoons extra virgin olive oil
1 teaspoon salt
1 1/2 cups all-purpose flour, plus a little more for kneading
1 cup stoneground whole wheat flour

1.  In a large bowl, combine the yeast, warm water, and sugar. Stir well with a fork and let sit for 10 minutes, until the mixture is frothy.

2.  Add the olive oil and salt. Stir in the flours, mixing to form a shaggy dough. Sprinkle a little flour onto a clean work surface, turn out the dough, and knead it for 3 to 4 minutes until smooth and springy. Return the dough to the mixing bowl and cover with plastic wrap. Let the dough rise at least 1 hour before using.

3.  To use the dough, preheat the oven to 475 degrees F. Sprinkle a work surface generously with flour. Divide dough in half and pat each half into a disk. Place each disk on a baking sheet and top with sauce. Bake for 10 minutes. Add the remaining toppings and bake an additional 10 minutes, until the cheese is melted.

# Making Dough

- Pizza crusts need a very hot oven. Turn the oven up as high as it will go. If you can heat your oven to 500 degrees F, your crust will be all the better for it.

- For a soft, damp dough (such as the no-knead type), sprinkle flour or cornmeal directly on the baking sheet and gently pat the dough into shape.

- Make sure your hands are clean, totally dry, and well dusted with flour.

- Work on a well-floured surface.

- Press down lightly and evenly on the ball of dough with the palms of your hands to start flattening it, working from the inside out toward the edges.

- Stretch and pull the dough carefully in opposite directions, working your way around and gently coaxing it outward, until the entire disk is about 1/4 to 1/8 of an inch thick.

- A well-kneaded, well-developed dough is easier to work, but don't be tempted to add extra flour. Dry dough is hard to stretch.

- If the dough keeps snapping back, let it rest for a few minutes, then start stretching it gently again.

- If you're having trouble flattening the dough evenly, use a rolling pin, but only as the last resort. It's better to use your hands to flatten pizza dough.

- Too lumpy or too many holes? Gather up the dough and press it gently into the bottom of a rimmed baking sheet to make a deep-dish style pizza.

# Peanut Noodles with Chicken and Cucumber

Given how simple this recipe is, the flavors are deep and complex. That's the fish sauce, which may smell a bit fishy in the bottle, but it disappears into any dish and adds a rich, almost meaty taste. Fish sauce is in the Asian section of nearly any supermarket.

*Makes 6 servings*

For the sauce:
1/3 cup coconut milk
1/3 cup water
1 cup natural peanut butter (smooth or chunky)
3 tablespoons fish sauce
2 tablespoons toasted sesame oil
1 tablespoon soy sauce
Juice of 1 lime
1 teaspoon hot sauce, such as Sriracha
1 garlic clove

For the noodles:
1 pound Chinese egg noodles (or thin spaghetti)
2 to 3 cups cooked chicken meat (from a 2-pound rotisserie chicken)
1 medium cucumber, peeled, seeded, and cut into matchsticks
3 scallions, thinly sliced
2 tablespoons chopped fresh cilantro
2 tablespoons chopped peanuts

1.  Put all the sauce ingredients in a blender or food processor in the order listed, and pulse until the sauce is smooth. Set aside at room temperature.

2.  Cook the Chinese egg noodles or spaghetti according to package directions. Rinse in cool water, draining well.

3.  In a large bowl, toss the noodles with the peanut sauce. Add the chicken and half the cucumbers, tossing to barely combine. Spoon into a deep serving platter and top with the remaining cucumber. Sprinkle with the scallions, cilantro, and chopped peanuts.

# Chicken-Coconut Curry

Curry sounds complex if you think of it as needing lots and lots of spices. But look for jars of curry paste in the Indian food section of your supermarket. You can double this recipe if your pan is big enough, or make two batches—it's easy! Serve with hot basmati or jasmine rice (or plain white rice, if you prefer).

*Makes 6 servings*

2 tablespoons olive oil
1 large onion, thinly sliced
4 garlic cloves, minced
1 2-inch knob fresh ginger, peeled and finely chopped
1 1/2 pounds boneless, skinless chicken breasts
    (about 4 large), cut into 1-inch pieces
4 tablespoons medium or mild curry paste
1 15-ounce can coconut milk
Juice of 1 lime
Salt to taste

1.   In a large skillet over medium heat, drizzle in the olive oil and cook the onion, garlic, and ginger until the onion is just tender, about 6 minutes.

2.   Push the onions to one side and add the chicken. Cook, stirring, until the chicken is no longer pink, about 8 minutes.

3.   Add the curry paste and cook for 2 minutes, stirring. Add the coconut milk and then fill the can with water and add the water to the pan. Bring to a boil, reduce heat, and simmer for 10 minutes, until sauce is slightly thickened and the chicken is cooked through.

4.   Just before serving, squeeze in the lime juice and stir to combine. Taste and add a bit of salt if needed.

# Pecan Toffee Bars

In a hurry but need to make dessert? You'll find yourself reaching for this recipe over and over again. It's one of those terrific dishes whose total is more than the sum of its parts, transforming a pack of graham crackers and some butter, sugar, and pecans into a delectable confection.

1 package graham crackers (9 rectangles)
1/2 cup whole pecans
1/2 cup (1 stick) salted butter
1/2 cup golden brown sugar
1 teaspoon vanilla

1. Preheat the oven to 350 degrees F and line a baking sheet with parchment or foil. (If using foil, butter it lightly.)
2. Break each graham cracker along its dotted lines into four small rectangles and lay them out on the baking sheet. Top each one with a whole pecan or a piece of a pecan.
3. In a medium saucepan over medium-high heat, melt the butter and sugar together. Bring to a full rolling boil, then remove from heat and stir in the vanilla.
4. Spoon the butter-sugar mixture over the graham crackers (if you simply pour it on from the pan, you risk washing the pecans right off the crackers). Bake for 10 minutes until the entire pan is bubbling. Remove to a cooling rack and leave to cool; set at room temperature.
5. When the toffee is completely set, break the crackers into individual pieces. They will come out as whole rectangles, with a crisp sheet of toffee around the edges of each piece. Store in an airtight container at room temperature, layering the crackers between sheets of waxed paper, for up to 1 week.

# Mini Chocolate Lava Cakes

What if the kind of molten chocolate cakes you get as dessert in a nice restaurant could become finger food? They can, if you use foil baking cups and don't serve them to your guests *too* hot. These little cakes highlight the flavor of the chocolate, even though they'll also be good with any ordinary chocolate chip. I like Ghirardelli's chocolate chips, which are readily available at any grocery store, but you can use 6 ounces of any dark chocolate you prefer.

*Makes 8 servings*

1/2 cup (1 stick) salted butter
1 cup semisweet chocolate chips
1/3 cup golden brown sugar
4 eggs
1/4 cup all-purpose flour

1.   Preheat the oven to 450 degrees F and line 8 muffin tins with foil muffin cups. Lightly butter the bottom of the muffin cups or spritz them lightly with a nonstick spray.
2.   In a microwavable glass bowl, melt butter and chocolate in the microwave on high for 1 minute. Stir and microwave again for 30 to 60 seconds if needed. Don't overheat. Any remaining chips will quickly melt in the hot butter.
3.   Stir in the sugar, then beat in the eggs. Stir in the flour and salt and divide the mixture among the muffin cups.
4.   Bake for 6 to 8 minutes, until the little cakes have risen and the top is just set. They should still be jiggly.
5.   Remove from the oven and let cool a bit before serving. They're best served just warm, but even though the cakes will firm up as they cool, they should still have a slightly runny center. Store leftovers in the refrigerator where they will firm into a terrific fudgy texture.

# CHAPTER 2

# MARCH MADNESS AND THE NBA FINALS

SPRING IS IN the air and the ball is in the net—March brings the culmination of basketball season, and that means zesty, lighter fare for your super sports fans. Pork roast barbecue with coleslaw is a perennial favorite in ACC territory, and it's an excellent way to feed a lot of people without spending all day in the kitchen. A huge pork roast can smoke on the grill all afternoon, ready to be meltingly tender and succulent when the first whistle blows.

Baked Jalapeño Crab Dip
Sticky Sweet and Sour Chicken Wings
Spicy Grilled Cheese Fingers
Pork Roast Barbecue
Grilled Pepperoni Pizza with Quick Dough
Grilled Fajita Tacos
Garlic Potato Planks
Chocolate and Peanut-Dipped Potato Chips
Nutty Fudge No-Crust Pie

# Baked Jalapeño Crab Dip

Crabmeat's delicate flavor can get buried if you mix in too many strong flavors. The creamy sauce in this dip has just a little bite from a fresh jalapeño, letting the finished dish highlight the sweet seafood instead. While fresh crabmeat is always delicious, this recipe works equally well with frozen and even canned crabmeat. Serve with salted white corn chips for guests on the run or with rounds of sliced baguette. With a glass of white wine and a green salad, this rich dip can become a light main course.

*Makes 6 servings*

1 8-ounce package cream cheese, softened
1 cup mayonnaise
1/4 cup buttermilk
Juice of 1 lemon
1/2 teaspoon salt
1 jalapeño, finely minced
1 pound lump crabmeat, picked over, any shells discarded
1 tablespoon onion powder
1 tablespoon hot sauce
1/4 cup grated Parmesan

1.   Preheat the oven to 350 degrees F and grease a 1-quart baking dish.
2.   In a mixing bowl, blend the cream cheese and mayonnaise with an electric mixer on medium speed. Blend in the buttermilk, lime juice, and salt until the mixture is smooth.
3.   Using a wooden spoon or rubber spatula, gently fold in the crabmeat. Turn the mixture into the prepared baking dish and sprinkle with the Parmesan. Bake for 30 minutes, until the mixture is golden and bubbling.

# Sticky Sweet and Sour Chicken Wings

Grilling up a mountain of chicken wings makes for an excellent pregame show, if you have some company to chat with while you drink a beer and hover over the grill. The sauce is simple here, because the real star is the smoky, meaty chicken wings. Grilling them long and slow lets all the fat drip out and really crisps up the skin. Ten pounds of wings sound like a lot, but it doesn't go as far as you may think once they're cooked into golden crispness.

*Makes 12 to 15 servings*

10 pounds chicken wings, trimmed and jointed
Salt and pepper
1 16-ounce jar apricot preserves
1/2 cup red wine vinegar
1/2 cup soy sauce
3 tablespoons sesame seeds

1.   Preheat a gas grill on high with the lid closed, for 10 minutes. Sprinkle the wings liberally with salt and pepper. Blend the apricot preserves, vinegar, soy sauce, and sesame seeds in a medium bowl and set it aside.
2.   Reduce the gas to medium and arrange the wings on the grill rack. Tend them for 45 minutes or up to an hour, turning the wings and moving them around the grill to avoid burning. Grill until they're crisp and browned and crunchy.
3.   When they look done, use a brush to spread the apricot mixture generously over the wings. Continue to cook for 10 minutes more, turning and brushing, until they're well glazed.
4.   Serve warm or at room temperature.

# Spicy Grilled Cheese Fingers

Grilled cheese, the favorite lunch of children, is also appealing to adults, particularly if you amp up the flavor with chipotle. The secret ingredient is the tangy spiced mayonnaise, used inside and outside the bread. It's much easier to spread than butter and helps make for a golden crust.

*To make 4 large sandwiches*

1 cup mayonnaise
1 chipotle in adobo, minced, plus 2 tablespoons adobo sauce
Juice of 1 lime
8 large slices bread
3 cups grated sharp cheddar

1.   In a small bowl, blend the mayo with the minced chipotle, adobo, and lime juice.

2.   Spread each slice of bread evenly on both sides with the mayonnaise mixture. Divide the cheese among four of the slices and top with the remaining slices.

3.   Heat a large skillet or griddle, preferably nonstick, over medium heat. Cook each sandwich for about 4 minutes, then flip and continue cooking 4 to 6 minutes, until the bread is golden brown and the cheese is melted.

4.   Remove the finished sandwich to a cutting board and let it stand for a moment before slicing into one-inch wide fingers with a serrated knife.

# Pork Roast Barbecue

In the summertime, all over North Carolina, you can smell home grillers cooking pork. Doing it yourself isn't quite the same as partaking of the excellent pitmaster restaurants that dot the area, where whole pigs have been cooking in underground pits overnight, but you can make a very impressive facsimile with a little time and patience and a gas grill with a lid. Don't rush it; the pork shoulder really needs to cook long and slow to get tender. Serve the shredded meat heaped onto soft hamburger buns with the extra sauce on the side and maybe a little coleslaw. It doesn't need anything else.

*Makes 10 to 12 servings*

1 7-pound pork shoulder, on the bone
Salt and pepper

For the sauce:
1 1/2 cups cider vinegar
1/2 cup ketchup
1 tablespoon paprika
2 teaspoons dry mustard powder
2 teaspoons hot sauce
1 teaspoon salt
1 teaspoon red pepper flakes

1.   Preheat a gas grill on high for 10 minutes with the lid down. Turn off one side and set a drip tray below the grill rack on the side that's off.
2.   Rub the pork shoulder liberally all over with salt and pepper. Lay it on the grill rack over the drip tray. Set the other burner to medium heat, and close the lid. If you have a thermometer on the grill, keep an eye on it to keep the

grill's temperature at around 400 degrees F. Cook for four hours with the lid down.

3.   While the roast is cooking, put the sauce ingredients in a small saucepan and bring to a boil, and let simmer for 3 to 4 minutes. Set aside to cool.

4.   After 4 hours, mop the roast all over with the sauce. (If the pork roast had its skin still on, it will pull off easily now; do that before mopping.) Close the lid and continue cooking, mopping frequently, for another 1 to 2 hours, until the meat is meltingly tender and can be pulled apart with two forks. If it's not (depending on your grill), keep mopping and cooking for another hour or so.

5.   Lift the roast onto a serving platter and pull all the meat off the bone. Shred it with two forks and season with a little more of the mopping sauce. Serve hot or at room temperature.

*Makes 8 servings*

10 cups shredded green cabbage (about 1/2 a large head)
2 large carrots, peeled and shredded
1/2 cup mayonnaise
1/4 cup sour cream
3 tablespoons white wine or apple cider vinegar
1 tablespoon yellow mustard
Salt and freshly ground black pepper

1.   Toss the cabbage and carrots together in a large mixing bowl.

2.   In a small bowl, whisk the mayonnaise and sour cream with the vinegar and mustard until smooth. Toss with the cabbage, and season to taste with a little salt, if needed, and a lot of black pepper. Cover and store as long as overnight before serving.

# Creamy Carolina Slaw

The smoky, tangy flavors of long-cooked pork barbecue are just begging for a creamy mayonnaise-based slaw to complement them. You can substitute buttermilk or plain yogurt (or plain Greek yogurt) for the sour cream, but the thickness of the cream helps this slaw hold up well on a buffet table without looking watery. It's best made the day before so the cabbage softens and the flavors meld. Just stir it up from the bottom before serving.

# Grilled Pepperoni Pizza with Quick Dough

There are a few secrets to grilling pizza, and a key one is not heating the grill too hot—you don't want the crust to char before the cheese can melt. Also, remember, less is more when it comes to grilled pizza toppings, so add the tomato sauce and cheese with a restrained hand.

*Makes 4 servings*

1 envelope active dry yeast
1 cup warm water
1 teaspoon sugar
2 tablespoons olive oil
1 teaspoon salt
2 1/4 cups all-purpose flour
1/4 cup cornmeal

For the pizza:
1/2 cup tomato sauce
1/2 teaspoon dried oregano
Olive oil
Sliced pepperoni
Grated mozzarella

1. To make the dough, put the yeast, water, and sugar in the bowl of a food processor and stir it together. Wait 5 minutes until the mixture is frothy. Add the olive oil, salt, flour, and cornmeal and pulse until a ball of dough comes together. Turn out the dough and knead three times. Use right away, or leave it in a bowl, covered with plastic wrap, to rise for an hour.

2. Preheat a gas grill for 10 minutes with the lid closed. In a small bowl, combine the tomato sauce with the oregano.

3. To make pizza, divide the dough into quarters and roll it into four thin circles about 6 inches across. Brush a little oil across the crust and then slide the crust onto the center of the grill, oiled side down. Cook for 2 minutes, until firmed up and crisp, then brush the top with olive oil and flip.

4. Pull the crust to the side of the grill with tongs. Working quickly, spread a little tomato sauce on the crust and sprinkle with pepperoni and cheese. Pull the pizza back toward the center with tongs, cover the grill, and cook 2 more minutes, until cheese is melting. Repeat with remaining ingredients.

# Grilled Fajita Tacos

If your fajitas don't taste like they do at a restaurant, it's because you're not using flank or skirt steak. Both have the chewy, intense beefiness that you get with a good restaurant version. It's crucial not to overcook either flank or skirt, however, and grilling really helps with that. Follow the timing below.

*Makes 6 servings*

2 pounds skirt or flank steak
2 tablespoons chili powder
1 teaspoon salt
2 tablespoons olive oil
1 large red bell pepper, thinly sliced
1 large green bell pepper, thinly sliced
1 large yellow onion, thinly sliced
2 garlic cloves, minced
Salt and pepper
12 8-inch flour tortillas, warmed
Salsa and sour cream

1.   Rub the steak all over with the chili powder and salt. Set it aside to marinate.

2.   Heat the olive oil in a large skillet over medium heat and add the onions, peppers, and garlic. Cook, stirring, until the vegetables are tender and the onions are translucent, about 6 to 8 minutes. Season with salt and pepper.

3.   Preheat a broiler or grill on high and cook the steak for 3 to 4 minutes, then turn and cook an additional 4 minutes. Allow the meat to rest 5 minutes, then slice thinly against the grain.

4.   Heap meat and peppers on warm tortillas and top with salsa and sour cream.

# Garlic Potato Planks

The sort of thick oven fries that you get at steakhouses aren't hard to make, but you can't be shy about the oil, or they won't bake to be properly golden and crisp outside with a tender, creamy interior. This recipe flavors the oil with garlic before baking, which prevents the garlic from scorching in the oven, but if you want to skip the microwave step, just sprinkle your potato planks with 1 teaspoon of garlic powder along with the salt and pepper.

*Makes 4 servings*

4 large Idaho baked potatoes
1/4 cup olive oil
4 cloves garlic, finely chopped
Salt and freshly ground black pepper

1.   Preheat the oven to 400 degrees F and lightly grease a large rimmed baking sheet. Scrub the potatoes, pat dry, and cut each one lengthwise into 8, 10, or 12 wedges, depending on the size of the potato (each wedge should be about 1/2 to 3/4 of an inch thick).

2.   Put the olive oil in a small microwavable bowl and add the garlic. Microwave on high for 1 1/2 minutes, until the oil is heated and the garlic is turning a little golden. Strain out and discard the garlic.

3.   Toss the potato wedges in the garlicky oil. Spread evenly on the baking sheet in a single layer and sprinkle generously with salt and pepper. Bake 15 minutes, then turn each wedge with a spatula, and cook another 10 minutes, until each potato plank is golden and tender.

# Chocolate and Peanut-Dipped Potato Chips

This is one of those ridiculously simple ideas that may even seem crazy—until you taste it. If you are one of those people who like the combination of sweet and salty—and so many of us are—you'll go nuts for this. Even though you have to individually dip each chip in the chocolate and nuts, the process goes quickly, and the results are really very impressive. You may not want to taste these while you're making them, or it will be hard to save any for your guests!

*Makes 8 to 10 servings*

2 cups roasted salted peanuts
1 12-ounce bag semisweet chocolate chips
1 6-ounce bag ridged potato chips

1.   Line a large baking sheet with waxed paper. Coarsely chop the peanuts and set aside in a small bowl.

2.   Melt the chocolate chips in the microwave for 1 minute on high, stirring well, then nuke for a couple 15-second bursts, stirring well after each, just until smooth. Don't overheat, or the chocolate will stiffen up and burn.

3.   Dip individual potato chips halfway into the chocolate, then sprinkle with chopped peanuts while the chocolate is still soft. Set the coated chips on the prepared baking sheet, and chill in the fridge till the chocolate is set. Store in an airtight container at room temperature for up to a week.

# Nutty Fudge No-Crust Pie

How does a no-crust chocolate pie differ from a pan of brownies? Well, it *is* similar, but when a brownielike mixture is baked in a pie pan, it's shallower, fudgier, and easily served in pielike wedges. The finished dessert eats like pie, and it's so rich and moist that you'll see right away it's not finger food. Have it warm or at room temperature, with a dollop of vanilla ice cream, if you like, but it's also good stored in the refrigerator and eaten cold and fudgy with a little whipped cream.

*Makes 8 servings*

1 stick butter
4 ounces dark chocolate (or 1 cup semisweet chocolate chips)
3/4 cup light brown sugar
2 eggs
2 egg yolks
2 tablespoons bourbon
1 teaspoon vanilla
1/4 cup flour
Pinch of salt
3/4 cup chopped walnuts or pecans

1.   Preheat the oven to 325 degrees F. Butter a 10-inch pie plate.
2.   Melt butter and chocolate in the microwave, stirring several times. Beat in the sugar, then add the eggs, yolks, and vanilla and mix well. Stir in the flour and salt just to combine, then add the nuts and stir.
3.   Turn the mixture into the prepared pan and bake for 18 to 20 minutes, just until the center is set.

# CHAPTER 3

# THE WORLD SERIES

BASEBALL SEASON MEANS summertime and foods that taste good in the great outdoors. And don't forget those ballpark classics like caramel corn with peanuts—it's even better if you make it yourself. The foods here are all ideal for an afternoon at your local ballpark, and if you're watching the game at home, why not spread a picnic blanket in front of the TV and make sure a shaft of sunlight is coming through the window?

Hot Garlic and Herb Potato Chips

Asian Peanut Slaw

Full-Meal Baked Beans

Fragrant Rice Pilaf with Butternut Squash

Chili Fries

Mini Cuban Sandwiches

Grilled Mexican Hot Dogs

Oven-Fried Ranch Chicken

Bacon and Buttermilk Biscuits

Homemade Caramel Corn

Apple Butter Hand Pies

# Hot Garlic and Herb Potato Chips

Hot potato chips with a garlicky and herb butter is the sort of snack that you might get when you order a glass of wine at a fancy restaurant bar. Those chips might have been made moments earlier by the chef and yes, they are delicious. But why do you have to get all dressed up and go out to enjoy such a treat? Why, in fact, do you even need to make potato chips? For this shortcut recipe, use the finest kettle chips you can buy—Cape Cod really *are* good—and salted butter for best results.

*Makes 8 servings*

1 9- or 10-ounce bag kettle potato chips, unflavored
1/4 cup (1/2 stick) salted butter
2 garlic cloves, minced
2 tablespoons finely chopped fresh parsley
1 tablespoon finely chopped fresh thyme leaves
Freshly ground black pepper

1.   Preheat the oven to 350 degrees F. Pour the chips on a large rimmed baking sheet and spread them into a single layer.

2.   In a small saucepan, put butter and minced garlic. Let it cook and melt slowly, stirring often, to infuse the garlic flavor into the butter. Stir in the chopped herbs and immediately pour the mixture evenly over the potato chips, tossing gently as needed to distribute the butter and herbs. Sprinkle with black pepper.

3.   Bake for 10 to 12 minutes, until the potato chips are hot throughout and have slightly absorbed the butter and herb mixture. Either serve from the hot baking sheet, or pour into a large serving dish. Eat hot, immediately.

# Asian Peanut Slaw

This Asian-inspired dressing, pungent with both fresh and ground ginger, makes a nice low-fat change from mayonnaise-dressed versions. It tastes even better after a couple days in the refrigerator. Food processors were made for slaw. You can reduce a head of cabbage to a quivering heap of shreds in about 30 seconds, whereas to achieve the same fineness with a knife takes a lot longer. If you want carrots, switch to the grating blade.

*Makes 8 servings*

6 cups finely shredded green cabbage (about 1/2 head)
4 cups finely shredded red cabbage (about 1/4 head)
2 medium carrots, grated
1/2 cup cider vinegar
3 tablespoons sesame oil
3 tablespoons soy sauce
1 tablespoon sugar
1 tablespoon ground ginger
1/2 cup salted peanuts
1/2 cup fresh cilantro

1.   In the bottom of a large mixing bowl, whisk the vinegar, sesame oil, soy sauce, sugar, and ginger in a small bowl. Add the cabbage and carrots and toss well to coat. Allow to sit at least 4 hours or as long as overnight.

2.   Just before serving, garnish with chopped, salted peanuts and cilantro.

# Full-Meal Baked Beans

These days, a lot of brands of baked beans come so elaborately flavored that the process of "doctoring" them up before heating is hardly necessary. But you can take them to a whole new level from a hearty side dish to a main course by adding even more. These beans start with the classic trinity of onions, carrot, and celery, lightly sautéed, along with diced bacon and big cubes of ham. The result, seasoned modestly with ketchup and yellow mustard for tanginess, is like the usual campfire baked beans, but bigger and better. Sometimes more really *is* more.

*Makes 8 servings*

6 slices thick-cut bacon, diced
1 medium onion, thinly sliced
1 medium carrot, diced
1 large celery stalk, thinly sliced
2 28-ounce cans baked beans
1 cup cubed ham
1/4 cup molasses
3 tablespoons ketchup
2 tablespoons yellow mustard

1.   Preheat the oven to 325 degrees F. In a Dutch oven or cast-iron stewpot, cook the bacon over medium heat, stirring often, until it is crisp and golden. Use a slotted spoon to lift it into a dish, and remove and discard all but 2 to 3 tablespoons of the bacon fat from the pan.
2.   Cook the onion, carrot, and celery in the bacon fat until onion is translucent, 7 to 8 minutes. Add the beans, ham, molasses, ketchup, and mustard. Reserve 2 tablespoons of the crisp bacon, put the rest in the pot, and stir.
3.   Bake for 30 minutes, until bubbling. Serve hot or warm.

# Fragrant Rice Pilaf with Butternut Squash

"White rice" is a synonym for "boring." This rice is anything but. It's a side dish that stands on its own, warm and fragrant with herbs. Remember to lift out the cinnamon stick before serving.

*Makes 6 servings*

3 tablespoons olive oil
1 medium yellow onion, thinly sliced
2 garlic cloves, minced
1 1/2 cups white rice
2 cups diced butternut squash (cut into 1/2-inch cubes)
1 cinnamon stick
1/4 teaspoon cumin seeds
1/4 teaspoon turmeric
1/4 teaspoon allspice
3 cups chicken stock (if using low-sodium stock,
    add 3/4 teaspoon salt)
1/2 cup raisins or golden raisins
3 tablespoons chopped fresh parsley
Freshly ground black pepper
Salt
Lemon wedges, for garnish

1.   Put the olive oil in a large, heavy skillet that has a lid. Cook the onions and garlic for 2 to 3 minutes, until the onions soften. Add the rice and cook, stirring, for 3 to 4 minutes, until the rice grains lightly brown. Add the squash cubes and cook for 2 minutes, stirring often, until the edges of some cubes are lightly browned.

2.   Add the cinnamon stick, cumin seeds, turmeric, allspice, and raisins and cook, stirring, for 1 minute. Pour in the chicken stock and stir in the raisins. Cover and cook 20 minutes, until the liquid has been absorbed. Taste and adjust seasoning, adding pepper and salt as needed, then sprinkle with parsley and serve with lemon wedges to squeeze over each serving.

# Chili Fries

What's a visit to the ballpark without an upside-down plastic baseball cap filled with hot fries, cheesy sauce, and a ladle of chili? What I don't love is the plastic fork, which feels so greasy while you're eating this classic treat. Using frozen french fries and a jar of cheese sauce (such as Cheez Whiz), this is a snap to make at home. If you have home-made chili, that's ideal, but it is also delicious with a good brand of canned chili with beans. You may be surprised at how much better it tastes in a bowl with a real metal fork.

*Makes 4 to 6 servings*

1 16-ounce bag frozen french fries
2 cups homemade chili, or 1 15-ounce can chili with beans
1 16-ounce jar cheese sauce, such as Cheez Whiz

1.   Bake the fries according to package directions. While they're cooking, heat the chili on the stovetop or in the microwave. Pour the cheese sauce in a bowl, cover with a plate, and microwave according to package directions until melted and smooth. (This makes for much easier cleanup than heating the cheese in a pot on the stovetop.)

2.   For each serving, mound a portion of fries on an indi-vidual plate or bowl, and top with cheese, then a dollop of chili. You can also heap all the fries onto a large serving platter and top with all the cheese—right out to the edges!—and then ladle the chili down the center. Eat at once before the fries get soggy.

# Mini Cuban Sandwiches

Cubanos, as lovers of these hefty sandwiches know them, tend to come large—a big roll, a lot of pork and ham, plenty of cheese, and a little mustard and pickles to cut the fat. It's a meal and then some, and it can be quite a commitment to finish one. Those flavors, right down to the pickle, remain just as good when shrunk down to slider size. These are easy to make without any home cooking, too: buy the ham, pork, and cheese already sliced at a deli, and all you have to do is turn on a skillet to toast them.

*Makes 12 sliders*

12 mini hamburger buns or slider rolls
Yellow mustard
12 slices pork
12 slices ham
12 slices Swiss or provolone cheese
Dill pickle slices
Mayonnaise or softened butter

1.  Lay out the rolls and spread a little mustard on the inside surfaces. Layer on the pork, ham, cheese, and pickles. Top with the other half of each roll. Spread a little mayo or softened butter on the outsides of each roll, top and bottom.
2.  Heat a large skillet, over medium heat. Fit the sandwiches, in batches, into the skillet, and press each one down very firmly with a spatula to crush the bread and filling as flat as you can. Fry on both sides, pressing firmly, until the bread is golden and the cheese is melted.
3.  Keep the finished sandwiches warm in a platter in a 180-degree F oven while you cook the remaining sandwiches. Serve with additional pickles and mustard.

# Grilled Mexican Hot Dogs

Ballpark dogs tend to be pretty plain and straightforward. This Tex-Mex variation on the theme is a classic in the American Southwest, where you can buy them from food trucks and dress your own with salsa and sour cream. For best results, buy the thinnest sliced bacon you can find; this is not the place to use thick-cut bacon, because it won't crisp up on the grill. Also, avoid maple- and brown sugar-flavored versions because the sugar is more likely to burn on the grill. The usual accompaniments are salsa and sour cream, but you can serve an array of toppings if you like, such as grated cheese, sliced scallions, and chopped fresh cilantro.

*Makes 8 dogs*

1 package hot dogs (8 dogs)
8 slices thin-cut bacon
8 hot dog buns
Salsa
Sour cream

1.  Preheat a gas grill on high for 10 minutes with the lid closed. While the grill is preheating, wrap each hotdog tightly with 1 strip of bacon, spiraling around the length of the frankfurter.
2.  Reduce the grill to medium and place the hot dogs over direct heat. Grill for 7 to 8 minutes, moving the hot dogs around frequently to prevent burning, until browned on all sides. For the last few minutes of grilling, open the buns and lay them face down over indirect heat to warm and lightly toast.
3.  Serve with salsa and sour cream for each diner to spoon over the hot dogs in the buns.

# Oven-Fried Ranch Chicken

Fried chicken is always a favorite on the buffet and picnic tables of sports fan, but yikes, it's a pain to fry it! The grease settles in a fine layer over the kitchen, and the house can smell like frying for days. Instead, use the oven, the perfect way to cook chicken through evenly, and if you line the baking sheet with foil, cleanup is a breeze—you can't say that about a skillet full of hot oil! The golden-brown crust from a homemade ranch seasoning (see the recipe on page 9) has lots of flavor, or you can use an envelope of commercial ranch dressing mix. This chicken is good hot or at room temperature.

*Makes 4 to 6 servings*

One 2 1/2- to 3-pound frying chicken, jointed into 8 pieces
1/3 cup Ranch Seasoning Blend (see page 9) or 1 envelope
    ranch dressing mix
Vegetable oil

1.   Cut the breasts in half to make 10 pieces. Put the chicken pieces in a gallon-size zipper locked bag and sprinkle it with the ranch seasoning. Seal the bag and massage the outside to make sure the chicken is completely coated in the mixture. Leave in the refrigerator to marinate at least 2 hours and preferably overnight.
2.   When ready to bake, preheat the oven to 350 degrees F and line a large, rimmed baking sheet with foil. Lightly oil the foil and arrange the chicken, skin-side up, on the baking sheet.
3.   Roast for 45 minutes, until the chicken is golden brown and cooked through. An instant-read thermometer inserted in the center of a thigh should read 180 degrees F. If not, give it 5 or 10 more minutes and check again.

# Bacon and Buttermilk Biscuits

Serve these tender biscuits with a big pot of chili or a stew. Use thick-sliced bacon for a real punch of smoky flavor.

*Makes 12 servings*

6 thick-cut bacon slices, diced
3 1/2 cups all-purpose flour
2 teaspoons baking powder
1 teaspoon baking soda
1 teaspoon salt
3/4 cup buttermilk
1/2 cup (1 stick) salted butter, melted
1 cup fresh corn kernels
1 cup grated sharp cheddar cheese
1/4 cup grated Parmesan
2 scallions, thinly sliced

1.  Preheat the oven to 425 degrees F. Fry the bacon pieces in a skillet over medium heat until crisp. Remove to a paper towel-lined plate with a slotted spoon and set aside.

2.  In a large mixing bowl, combine the flour, baking powder, baking soda, and salt. Make a well in the center and pour in the buttermilk and melted butter. Stir just to combine. Add the bacon, corn, cheese, Parmesan, and scallions.

3.  Drop the dough by big heaping spoonfuls onto an ungreased baking sheet, leaving at least 1 1/2 inches between biscuits.

4.  Bake 16 to 18 minutes, until puffed and golden and a tester in the center comes out clean. Serve hot.

# Homemade Caramel Corn

This treat is like ballpark caramel corn, but it outshines the purchased version because it's both tender and crisp. A candy thermometer and a heatproof silicone spatula make it super-easy.

*Makes about 8 cups*

8 cups freshly popped popcorn (from 1/2 cup kernels)
1 cup dry-roasted salted peanuts
1/2 teaspoon baking soda
1/2 cup (1 stick) butter
2 cups firmly packed brown sugar
2 tablespoons light corn syrup

1.   Put the popcorn in a large, heatproof bowl with the peanuts.
2.   Liberally grease a large, rimmed baking sheet. Measure the baking soda and set it in a small dish by your workspace.
3.   Combine the butter, sugar, and corn syrup in a large, heavy-bottomed saucepan and bring to a boil over medium heat, stirring constantly until the sugar dissolves.
4.   Without stirring, boil 5 to 10 minutes until it reaches 300 degrees F on a candy thermometer. Immediately remove the pan from the heat, add the baking soda, and stir briskly. Pour the caramel over the popcorn and mix.
5.   Quickly pour the caramel corn onto the prepared baking sheet and spread it out to cool. (The process from the time the caramel reaches 300 degrees F through spreading the mixture on the baking sheet should take 1 minute.) When fully cool, break it into large chunks. Store in an airtight container for up to 1 week.

# Apple Butter Hand Pies

What's baseball without apple pie? Hardly imaginable. These apple hand pies are filled with tangy, dark, spicy apple butter, which makes things much easier on the cook, who doesn't have to peel all those apples, and it's a nice change from the usual flavors.

*Makes 6 servings*

1 1/4 cups all-purpose flour
2 tablespoons sugar, plus more for sprinkling
1/2 teaspoon salt
1/2 cup (1 stick) unsalted butter, cold
3 tablespoons ice water
6 to 8 tablespoons commercially prepared apple butter
1 egg, beaten

1.   Put the flour, sugar, salt, and butter in a food processor and pulse until it resembles cornmeal. With the machine running, add the ice water all at once and process until the dough gathers into a ball. Turn the dough onto a sheet of plastic wrap. Press into a disk and refrigerate for 30 minutes.

2.   When ready to assemble, preheat the oven to 425 degrees F and line a baking sheet with parchment paper or lightly buttered foil (not wax paper). Divide the dough into 6 balls. On a lightly floured surface, roll each ball into a circle about 5 inches in diameter.

3.   Put a heaping tablespoon of apple butter in the center of each circle and fold the dough over into a half-moon shape. Use a fork to press all around the outside edges to seal, and then use the fork to poke a few vent holes in the top crust.

4.   Brush the top with beaten egg and sprinkle with sugar. Bake 10 to 12 minutes, until golden brown.

CHAPTER 4

# THE STANLEY CUP

Hockey season doesn't get as much play at home events because passionate fans like to see all the action happening on the ice. If you're watching on TV, you might look away and miss a major pileup on the rink. But make it a family event by having your friends around for lots of puck-shaped food and many other delicious things!

Cross-Check Hot-Seasoned Nuts

Zucchini-Parmesan Pucks

Baba Ghanoush with Pomegranate

Chicken Nuggets with Wasabi Maple Mustard

Back-of-the-Net Pork and Beef Chili

Cheddar and Scallion Corn Muffins

Chipotle Chicken Sliders

Cold Box No-Boil Fudge

Miracle Microwave Peanut Brittle

# Cross-Check Hot-Seasoned Nuts

Passengers flying in business class are often treated to a dish of hot-seasoned mixed nuts while they sit and drink their champagne, and the rest of us shuffle by to the more crowded section in the rear, where no warm snacks await us. So, your guests may appreciate the extra effort you've made by treating them to a first-class bowlful of hot-seasoned nuts. It's surprisingly simple, more than the sum of its parts. Don't skimp on the cayenne, which gives them zing.

*Makes 8 to 10 servings*

4 cups mixed nuts
1/4 cup (1/2 stick) salted butter
3 tablespoons chopped fresh rosemary leaves
1 teaspoon ground cayenne (or to taste)
Salt and freshly ground black pepper

1.   Preheat the oven to 350 degrees F and pour the nuts onto a rimmed baking sheet. In a small saucepan (or in a bowl in the microwave), melt the butter. Whisk in the rosemary and cayenne and a dash of salt and several grindings of pepper.

2.   Pour this mixture over the nuts and toss well to combine.

3.   Bake the nuts for 10 minutes, opening the oven to shake the baking sheet every few minutes to distribute the butter mixture. Pour the nuts into a large serving dish and serve hot, immediately.

# Zucchini-Parmesan Pucks

Hard to argue with a green vegetable when it's fried, right? And hardened hockey fans will especially love the fact that these come shaped just like little pucks. Kids and adults go nuts for these cheesy little pancakes. They're sort of like fried potato cakes—but with zucchini, which gives them a mild sweetness and harmonizes well with the Parmesan cheese. Served hot with a dollop of cold sour cream, they're a great appetizer.

*Makes 6 servings*

Vegetable oil for frying
3 medium zucchini, shredded
3 scallions, thinly sliced
1/2 cup grated Parmesan
1/2 cup all-purpose flour
1 egg, beaten
1/4 teaspoon salt
1/4 teaspoon freshly ground black pepper
Sour cream, for serving

1.  Preheat the oven to 180 degrees F. Heat 1/4 inch of vegetable oil in a large skillet over medium heat. While the oil heats, stir the zucchini, scallions, Parmesan, flour, salt, and pepper together. Add the egg, and mix to combine.
2.  Drop large spoonsful of the mixture into the hot oil, being careful not to overcrowd the pan, and flatten each pancake slightly with the back of the spoon.
3.  Cook for about 3 minutes, then flip and continue cooking until crisp and golden, 2 to 3 more minutes. Remove to an ovenproof serving plate and place in the preheated oven. Continue cooking, transferring each puck to the oven. Serve hot, with sour cream.

# Baba Ghanoush with Pomegranate

The garlicky roasted eggplant dip known as baba ghanoush is nearly as common as hummus these days. To liven it up, don't skimp on the lemon, and do add some pomegranate molasses! This deep red syrup is the result of boiling down pomegranate juice. It adds a sweet-tart flavor all its own, making this an excellent spread for slices of French bread, toasted pita, or blanched vegetables, such as cauliflower and broccoli.

*Makes 6 to 8 servings*

1 large eggplant
1/3 cup tahini
1/4 cup water
1 garlic clove, minced
3 tablespoons pomegranate molasses
Juice of 1 lemon
Salt and pepper
1/2 cup pomegranate seeds
3 tablespoons olive oil

1.   Place the eggplant directly over a gas flame on your stovetop or outdoor grill and cook it, turning frequently, until the outside is blackened and charred and the eggplant starts to collapse because the inside is tender. Move it to a plate and cool.

2.   When cool enough to handle, slice it open and scoop the tender flesh into a wire mesh strainer, discarding the skin. Let it drain over a sink for 10 minutes.

3.   Turn the drained eggplant into a mixing bowl and use a whisk to mix it vigorously with the tahini and water to make it fluffy and smooth. Add the garlic, pomegranate molasses, lemon, salt, and pepper and stir.

4.   Stir in the pomegranate seeds and spoon the baba ghanoush onto a serving plate. Drizzle with olive oil and serve.

# Chicken Nuggets with Wasabi Maple Mustard

Chicken nuggets become very much grown-up food in these delicate, crisp little bites. Panko bread crumbs are perfect here; don't use freshly made soft crumbs or the nuggets won't be as crisp. Don't overheat the oil; 275 degrees F is about hot enough so they cook without burning. They're also good with a splash of commercially made sweet chili sauce.

*Makes 6 servings*

For the dipping sauce:
1/2 cup yellow mustard
2 tablespoons maple syrup
1 teaspoon wasabi powder

For the nuggets:
4 large boneless, skinless chicken breasts
Vegetable oil for frying
1/2 cup all-purpose flour
Salt and pepper
2 eggs, beaten with 1 tablespoon water
2 to 3 cups dry bread crumbs

1.   Cut the chicken breasts into bite-size pieces and heat 3/4 inch of oil to about 275 degrees F in a large deep skillet over medium heat. Preheat the oven to 180 degrees F and line an ovenproof serving platter with paper towels.
2.   Put the flour, eggs, and bread crumbs in three separate shallow bowls. Dip the chicken in the flour, then the egg, then the crumbs, and then lay those pieces directly in the hot oil. Cook 2 to 3 minutes, turn, and cook an additional 3 minutes until the nuggets are golden.
3.   Remove to the serving platter in the oven and continue with the remaining chicken. Serve hot with dipping sauce.

# Back-of-the-Net Pork and Beef Chili

This man-style chili features no beans and a complex flavor based on guajillo and chipotle chilies, both usually available in the Mexican section of a big supermarket. To serve, put out a big bowl of corn chips and let each guest put a handful of chips in a serving bowl before ladling on a generous portion of chili directly over their chips. Toppings such as cheese and chopped scallions are good, but a dollop of sour cream may be all you need.

*Makes 8 servings*

6 guajillo chilies, stems and seeds removed
1 1/2 cups boiling water
6 fresh tomatillos, papery outer layer discarded
6 garlic cloves, unpeeled
2 chipotle chiles in adobo
2 tablespoons olive oil
2 large yellow onions, diced

2 1/2 pounds beef chuck, diced into 1 1/2 inch cubes
1 large onion, diced
4 garlic cloves, minced
1 15-ounce can diced tomatoes
2 tablespoons ancho chile powder
2 teaspoons ground cumin
1 1/2 teaspoons salt

1.  In a dry skillet over medium heat, toast the guajillo chilies on each side for 30 seconds, until just softened. Put them in a glass bowl and pour boiling water over them to cover. Soak for 15 minutes.
2.  In the same dry skillet, toast the tomatillos and garlic, turning several times until the vegetables have softened slightly and the exteriors have brown marks, for 3 to 4 minutes. Discard the paper skins on the garlic.
3.  Put the guajillo chilies in a blender with the soaking water, the tomatillos, the peeled garlic, and the chipotle chilies in adobo. Pulse to make a smooth puree.
4.  In a large stewpot over medium heat, cook the onions until softened and just turning golden, 6 to 7 minutes. Add the beef and cook through, about 10 minutes.
5.  Add the pureed chiles and tomatillos, the tomatoes, ancho powder, cumin, and salt. Bring to a boil, reduce heat, and simmer gently for 1 hour, stirring now and then, until the sauce thickens.

# Cheddar and Scallion Corn Muffins

Adding fresh corn kernels (you can use frozen), sharp cheddar, and chopped scallions makes corn muffins moist and full of flavor. They're so good that you could serve them as an appetizer, perhaps with a dish nearby of softened butter blended with a little honey.

*Makes 18 muffins*

1 1/2 cups stoneground cornmeal
1/2 cup all-purpose flour
3 teaspoons baking powder
1/2 teaspoon baking soda
1 teaspoon salt
1 1/2 cups buttermilk

1/2 cup (1 stick) salted butter, melted
2 eggs
1 cup grated sharp cheddar
1 cup fresh corn kernels
4 scallions, thinly sliced

1. Preheat the oven to 425 degrees F and line 18 muffin tins with foil or paper wrappers.

2. In a large bowl, blend the cornmeal, flour, baking powder, soda, and salt. In a small bowl, whisk the melted butter with the buttermilk and eggs. Make a well in the center of the dry ingredients and pour in the liquid. Stir just to combine. Add the cheese, corn, and scallions, and stir just to combine.

3. Divide the batter among the prepared muffin tins and bake 18 to 20 minutes, or until a toothpick pushed into the center comes out with a few crumbs clinging to it.

# Chipotle Chicken Sliders

If you prep all the ingredients, you can double or triple this recipe, lay out all the pieces, and let guests prep their own, so that each delectable little sandwich is freshly made. But with all this luscious sauce to soak into the buns, these are also delicious made as much as an hour in advance. Put two toothpicks through each slider, and you can cut the sandwiches in half, so guests can see the layers of filling, as you arrange the cut sliders on a serving platter.

*Makes 8 servings*

For the sauce:
1/2 cup mayonnaise
1/2 cup sour cream
3 tablespoons chopped canned chipotle chiles in adobo sauce
Juice and zest of one lime

For the sliders:
2 large boneless, skinless chicken breasts
Salt and freshly ground black pepper
1 teaspoon cumin
1 ripe Hass avocado
Juice of 1 lime
8 mini hamburger buns
Olive oil
1 15-ounce can refried beans
8 ounces mozzarella cheese, grated (about 2 cups)
Sliced ripe tomato
Thinly sliced lettuce
Fresh cilantro leaves

1.  Make the sauce: Puree the mayonnaise, sour cream, chipotle, and lime juice and zest in a blender until smooth, scraping down the sides once or twice. Transfer to a bowl and refrigerate.

2.  Preheat a gas grill with the lid down for 10 minutes on high. Split each chicken breast in half horizontally, and lay each piece between two pieces of plastic wrap. Pound each breast half until it's one-quarter inch thick (if you don't have a meat pounder, use the bottom of a small saucepan). Sprinkle with salt, pepper, and cumin on each side.

3.  Mash the avocado with the lime juice and season with salt, and warm the refried beans on the stovetop or in the microwave.

4.  Grill the chicken breasts for 4 to 5 minutes, turning once. Set aside and keep warm. Split the buns and brush lightly with olive oil. Grill, cut sides down, until just golden brown, about a minute. Remove to a platter and cut each into four quarters.

5.  To assemble each sandwich, spread the bottom half of each toasted roll with a quarter of the mashed avocado. Top with a chicken breast quarter, then spoon on a quarter of the refried beans. Divide the cheese among the sandwiches, and top with tomato, lettuce, and a sprinkle of cilantro. Drizzle on a generous amount of the sauce and top with the remaining bun half. Cut each sandwich in half before serving.

# Tips for Better Sliders

1. Use a soft bun. Chewy bread, such as a good bakery sourdough roll, is delicious, but not ideal for a sandwich this small: the filling is too likely to squeeze out if people have to tear at the bread with their teeth! Some supermarkets now sell small buns marked for making sliders.

2. Use a lot of filling and sauce! Conversely, sliders are tastiest when they're overfilled, moist, and messy. This kind of sandwich is too small for a discreet bit of meat and cheese. Stuff them full.

3. Go for big flavors. Each bite of these little gems should pack a wallop of flavor. The potent chipotle sauce on these chicken sliders would make a perfect topping for a mini hamburger too.

4. When in doubt, use a toothpick. Your overfilled, saucy sliders may slide around, and you don't want them falling apart on a party platter. Keep each one intact with a sandwich toothpick, but use the party kind with a cellophane frill, so that guests know each toothpick is there.

# Cold Box No-Boil Fudge

You can use any kind of nuts you like for a different flavor—try almonds, pecans, or peanuts—or swap out one cup of nuts for a cup of mini marshmallows to make a Rocky Road version. It's a very forgiving fudge, and all it asks is that you not microwave the chocolate for too long and scorch it.

*Makes 64 1-inch squares*

3 cups (1 1/2 12-ounce bags) semisweet chocolate chips
1 14-ounce can sweetened condensed milk
1/2 teaspoon salt
2 cups chopped walnuts
2 teaspoons vanilla

1.   Line an 8×8-inch pan with waxed paper, letting an inch or so overhang on either side for lifting later. Put the chocolate chips in a large microwavable bowl and heat on high for 90 seconds. Remove and stir well. Let the chips rest for a minute or two, stirring often. The residual heat will continue to melt them. If you need more time, microwave in 10-second bursts, stirring well after each burst.

2.   Add the sweetened condensed milk, salt, and vanilla and beat with a fork or a whisk until smooth. Stir in the chopped nuts and turn the mixture in to the prepared pan.

3.   Refrigerate until firm, about 1 hour. Use the waxed paper to lift the fudge onto a cutting board, and cut it into 8 slices by 8 slices to make 64 small squares. Store in the refrigerator for up to a week.

# Miracle Microwave Peanut Brittle

Don't use dry-roast peanuts for this recipe; the coating on them isn't ideal for peanut brittle. Roasted salted peanuts, the kind that look a little oily, are what you want here for the best flavor and appearance.

*Makes 1 pound peanut brittle*

1 cup salted peanuts
1 cup sugar
1/2 cup light corn syrup
4 tablespoons (1/2 stick) salted butter, plus more for greasing
1 teaspoon vanilla
1 teaspoon baking soda

1.   Lightly grease a rimmed baking sheet with butter. In a medium, microwavable bowl, stir together the peanuts, sugar, and corn syrup.
2.   Microwave for 4 minutes on high. Stir well, then nuke it for 3 more minutes.
3.   Add the butter and the vanilla, stirring until the butter is melted. Microwave for 90 seconds more, until the mixture is very hot. It may be bubbling a little.
4.   Add the baking soda and stir to combine—be careful when stirring not to splash it! Hot sugar burns. The mixture will foam up. Pour the mixture onto the prepared baking sheet. (A heatproof silicone spatula is ideal for this job.) Let it cool at room temperature for 1 hour, until the brittle is hard. If it isn't entirely cool, you can put it in the freezer for 10 minutes, but don't try to let it cool in there the whole time—the air in the fridge and freezer is too humid to let the sugar set up.
5.   Bread the sheet of peanut brittle into bite-size pieces, and store it in an airtight container for up to a week.

# CHAPTER 5

# THE SUPER BOWL

IF YOU'RE ONLY going to have people over for one sports event all year, then that event is probably going to be the Super Bowl. People who couldn't care less who's playing will still show up for a party on that particular Sunday evening, and you don't want anyone to go home hungry. Fancy food is *not* what you want here; instead, aim for hearty, satisfying, delicious, and maybe just a little out of the ordinary. For example, potato chips are always welcome, but don't open an envelope of onion soup mix to make onion dip for them. Instead, spend a little time caramelizing sliced onions in a skillet, and you'll end up with onion dip that will have people turning away from the big screen to look for more—that's the hallmark of good Super Bowl food!

Real Onion Dip
Fried Shrimp Wontons
Broccoli Slaw with Bacon
Bourbon Barbecue Meatballs
Baked Chilaquiles
Southwestern Pita Pizza
Grilled Baby Back Ribs with Smoky BBQ Dry Rub
Baked Chiles Rellenos
Pot Roast Beef Sandwiches
The Chewiest Peanut Butter Cookie
Salted Caramel Blondies

# Real Onion Dip

The fresh and potent flavors in this creamy dip will be a revelation if you thought homemade onion dip starts with a package of soup mix. This dip is delicious with raw vegetables—even as simple as baby carrots and celery sticks—but it really shines with potato chips. Don't rush frying the onions; let them get brown and tender slowly. That's where the flavor happens. If you want to doctor this dip up further, add 1/2 cup of crumbled blue cheese along with the onions.

*Makes about 2 1/2 cups*

3 tablespoons extra virgin olive oil
2 large yellow onions, thinly sliced
1 cup sour cream
1 cup mayonnaise
2 tablespoons Worcestershire sauce
2 teaspoons hot sauce (or to taste)
1/2 teaspoon ground black pepper

1.   Put the olive oil into a skillet over medium heat and cook the onions until they're deeply golden brown, about 30 minutes. Stir occasionally with a wood or metal spatula, and cook until the onions are deeply golden, brown, and caramelized—roughly 40 or 50 minutes, keeping the heat low so they don't burn. Set aside and let cool.
2.   Stir together the remaining ingredients. Add the cooled onions and taste, adding a bit more hot sauce or Worcestershire if you like.

# Fried Shrimp Wontons

If you can enlist friends or family to help fold the wontons, the filling is fast to make and the frying goes quickly at the end. And nothing smells more delicious than to come into a kitchen where something is frying! Serve these as an appetizer as soon as people come in the door, an indicator that there is lots of good food to come this particular Super Bowl evening.

*Makes about 60 wontons*

For the dipping sauce:
1/4 cup soy sauce
1/4 cup rice wine vinegar (or apple cider vinegar)
2 tablespoons water
1 teaspoon brown sugar
1 teaspoon toasted sesame oil
1 teaspoon red pepper flakes

For the wontons:
2 tablespoons olive oil
2 tablespoons finely chopped fresh ginger (about a 1-inch knob)
3 garlic cloves, minced
4 scallions, finely chopped
1 medium carrot, peeled and grated
4 cups thinly sliced napa cabbage (about 1/4 head)
1/2 pound peeled and deveined shrimp, chopped
2 tablespoons soy sauce
2 teaspoons toasted sesame oil
1/4 teaspoon red pepper flakes
1 package round wonton wrappers (usually about 60 wrappers)
Vegetable oil

1.   Whisk the dipping sauce ingredients together in a small bowl and set aside.

2.   Heat the oil in a large skillet over medium heat and add the ginger, garlic, scallions, and carrot. Cook for 1 minute, until fragrant. Stir in the cabbage and cook 3 to 4 minutes to wilt and soften. Push the vegetable mixture to one side and add the shrimp to the empty side. Cook 2 to 3 minutes, just until pink. Stir the shrimp into the cabbage, add the soy sauce, sesame oil, and red pepper flakes, and turn the mixture into a bowl to cool slightly.

3.   Fill a small dish with water and lay a wrapper on a clean work surface in front of you. Put a scant tablespoon of the filling in the center. Dip your fingertip in the water and run it around the outer edge of the wrapper. Fold it in half, pressing outward to release any air, and push down firmly to seal into a half-moon shape.

4.   Lay the finished wonton on a clean baking sheet and repeat. The wontons can touch, but don't stack them, or they'll stick together as they soften.

5.   To cook, heat 1 inch of oil in the bottom of a large skillet over medium high heat, until it reaches 350 degrees F on a cooking thermometer. Add the wontons, in batches, and cook until golden brown, about 2 to 3 minutes. Remove to a paper towel-lined serving platter and keep warm while you continue cooking the rest. Serve warm with the dipping sauce.

# Tips for Better Wontons

1.  Don't overfill! Less is more when it comes to wontons. Overfilling them makes them burst when cooking.

2.  Press out the air as you seal them. Fold each one over and push down gently around the filling so you avoid air pockets that might make them burst later.

3.  Don't use too much water to seal. Just dip your finger and dampen the edge of the wrappers. Don't use a brush, which makes them too wet, and they won't hold together as well.

4.  Avoid overcrowding the pan. Trying to put too many wontons in at one time means that each one won't get as evenly brown as it should.

5.  Add a frill. If you're feeling confident about your wrapping skills, you can make these look more elaborate and restaurant-style by slightly pleating the damp edges as you fold them together. Make the first seal, then crimp the edges together, gathering it into a pleat, and pressing down each pleat to seal. It's not necessary, but it gives your dumplings a professional look!

# Broccoli Slaw with Bacon

Not a lot of greenery appears on the average Super Bowl table, but this slaw is a good reason to make an exception. It's crunchy and sweet, salty and creamy, and still tastes terrific the next day, in the unlikely event that you have any leftovers. If you have a food processor with a slicing blade, that's the ideal way to cut the broccoli—fine, but not too fine.

*Makes 6 to 8 servings*

4 slices thick-cut bacon, diced
1 large head broccoli, coarsely shredded
1 cup finely shredded fresh kale leaves
1/2 cup dried cranberries or golden raisins
1/4 cup chopped toasted pecans or walnuts
4 scallions, thinly sliced

For the dressing:
1/2 cup mayonnaise
1/2 cup buttermilk
2 tablespoons apple cider vinegar
2 scallions, thinly sliced
Salt and fresh ground black pepper

1.   Fry the bacon in a skillet over medium heat until crisp. Set on a paper towel-lined plate to drain. In a large bowl, toss the broccoli and kale with the cranberries, nuts, and scallions.

2.   In a medium bowl, whisk the mayo, buttermilk, and vinegar until smooth. Add the scallions and season with salt and black pepper to taste. Pour over the salad and toss to combine. Let sit at least 30 minutes before serving, or covered, in the refrigerator, as long as overnight.

3.   Just before serving, toss with 3/4 of the bacon, and sprinkle the remaining bacon on top.

# Bourbon Barbecue Meatballs

The taste of bourbon isn't strongly evident in the sauce, which just slicks the meatballs and doesn't coat them heavily. Serve with toothpicks alongside, for the meatballs to be picked up as a snack, or with a big bowl of mashed potatoes as a delectable main dish.

*Serves 8*

1 cup soft, fresh bread crumbs
1/2 cup buttermilk
1 egg
2 tablespoons olive oil
1 large yellow onion, finely chopped
2 garlic cloves, minced
1 pound ground beef
1 pound ground pork
1 1/2 teaspoons salt
1/2 teaspoon freshly ground black pepper
1/4 cup (1/2 stick) salted butter
1 16-ounce bottle mild barbecue sauce
1/4 cup bourbon

1.   In a large mixing bowl, stir the bread crumbs with the cream and egg. Set aside for 10 minutes.

2.   Heat the olive oil in a large skillet over medium heat and cook the onion and garlic for 5 to 6 minutes until softened and slightly browned. Set the skillet aside without washing.

3.   Add the onions, beef, pork, salt, and pepper to the mixing bowl. Mix well—clean hands are best for this job. Roll into about 48 meatballs about 1 1/4 inches in diameter.

4.   In the same skillet, melt half the butter over medium-high heat. Cook in batches, turning gently, 6 to 8 minutes, adding more butter as needed, until cooked through.

5.   When all the meatballs are cooked, heat the barbecue sauce in the skillet, scraping up the pan drippings. Stir in the bourbon. Return all the meatballs to the pan and bring the sauce to bubbling, tossing the meatballs to heat through before serving.

# Baked Chilaquiles

Chilaquiles [chee-la-KEE-lays] is a classic, soupy, Mexican main dish originally developed as a way for the frugal cook to use up leftover tortillas. Fried in strips and tossed with a spicy sauce, they were hearty and filling and immensely satisfying. But the easiest way to make chilaquiles is with a bag of crunchy tortilla chips and a rotisserie chicken. Then it's short work to make a casserole that is still delicious even as it cools on your buffet table.

*Makes 6 to 8 servings*

1 10-ounce bag tortilla chips
8 ounces Monterey Jack cheese, shredded
3 cups shredded cooked chicken
1 teaspoon whole dried oregano leaves
1 teaspoon ground cumin
1 teaspoon chili powder
3 cups chicken stock
1 16-ounce container sour cream
1 16-ounce jar salsa, any variety
Juice of 1 lime

1.   Preheat the oven to 350 degrees F and lightly oil a 9 x 13-inch baking dish. In a large mixing bowl, combine the chips, shredded cheese, chicken, oregano, cumin, chili powder, and chicken stock.

2.   Spread the mixture into the prepared baking dish. Spoon 1 1/2 cups of sour cream over the top, smoothing it toward the edges. Pour the salsa over the sour cream.

3.   Bake for 25 minutes, until bubbling.

4.   While the casserole bakes, stir the lime juice into the remaining 1/2 cup of sour cream. Remove the casserole from the oven, and drizzle the sour cream and lime over the top.

# Southwestern Pita Pizza

Tomato and mozzarella are not the only flavor game in town when it comes to pizza. Southwestern flavors can totally rock a pie. Skip the tomato sauce in favor of a spicy mole sauce, and use whole wheat or white pita for the base. The beauty of these individual pizzas for a crowd is that you can assemble a pizza bar with all the toppings and let each guest make his or her own. Keep the oven hot and slide trays in and out for a quick bake as often as you like until everyone is full.

*For each serving:*

1 6-inch pita
3 tablespoons mole sauce
1/4 cup grated pepper jack cheese
3 tablespoons shredded cooked chicken
Salsa, sour cream, and sliced green onion for garnish

1.   Preheat the oven to 375 degrees and place the pita on a baking sheet. Spoon on the mole, swirling it with the back of the spoon to cover the pita to the edges. Top with the cheese.

2.   Sprinkle the chicken over the top and bake for 10 minutes, until the cheese is melting and the pita and chicken are heated through. Remove to a serving plate and top with a spoonful of salsa and sour cream in the center. Sprinkle on green onion and serve at once.

# Grilled Baby Back Ribs with Smoky BBQ Dry Rub

The best dry rub mixes are the ones you make yourself—you can adjust the flavors as you prefer. Ideally, rub the spice over the entire rack of ribs the day before you want to cook them.

*Makes 6 to 8 servings*

2 3-pound racks pork baby back ribs (about 12 ribs), trimmed, skin removed
3 tablespoons chili powder
2 tablespoons smoked paprika
2 tablespoons sweet paprika
1 tablespoon garlic powder
2 teaspoons salt
1 teaspoon ground cumin
1/2 teaspoon cayenne pepper
1/4 teaspoon ground cloves

1. Place the ribs in a 9 x 13-inch casserole dish. Combine all the spices in a small bowl and rub the exterior of the ribs all over with all the rub. Leave the ribs uncovered in the refrigerator for at least two hours and preferably overnight.

2. When ready to cook, preheat a gas grill on high for 10 minutes with the lid closed. Lay the ribs directly on the grill rack.

3. Grill for 45 to 60 minutes with the lid down, turning the ribs occasionally and moving them around now and then so they don't scorch.

# Baked Chiles Rellenos

The typical chiles rellenos found in a restaurant are roasted poblano chiles stuffed with meat and cheese, dipped in a batter and deep-fried. They're delicious—but you need to set aside the best part of an afternoon to make them! This streamlined version won't look anything like the restaurant type, but it's perhaps even more delicious, and much, much easier to make for a crowd. Look for whole roasted chiles in cans in the Mexican food aisle of your supermarket. If you want to double this recipe, bake it in a 9 x 13-inch casserole.

*Makes 6 servings*

1 pound lean ground beef
2 teaspoons chili powder
1 teaspoon dried whole oregano leaves
1 cup crushed tomatoes
2 7-ounce cans whole roasted chiles, drained
1 16-ounce jar medium salsa, any variety
8 ounces cheddar or Pepper Jack cheese, shredded (about 2 cups)

1.   Preheat the oven to 350 degrees F. Brown the hamburger in a large skillet over medium-high heat, breaking it up as you cook, until cooked through, about 6 to 8 minutes. Add the chili powder, oregano, and crushed tomato and cook until slightly thickened, about 5 minutes.
2.   Fill each chili with the meat mixture, and lay them in a single layer in a 2-quart baking dish. Spoon any remaining meat over the top of the chiles. Pour the salsa evenly over the chiles.
3.   Sprinkle with cheese and bake for 25 minutes, until the sauce is bubbling and the cheese is melted and browned.

# Pot Roast Beef Sandwiches

Pot-roast a big chunk of beef until it's meltingly tender, floating in its own brown gravy, to be heaped high on fluffy sandwich rolls. You won't need any other condiment, but you will need lots of napkins.

*Makes 8 to 10 servings*

1 4 1/2- to 5-pound chuck roast
1/4 cup flour
Salt and pepper
1/4 cup vegetable oil
1 large sweet onion, thinly sliced
6 garlic cloves
4 cups beef stock or water
8 to 10 large soft sandwich rolls

1.   Preheat the oven to 350 degrees F. Rub the chuck roast with the flour and liberally sprinkle it with salt and pepper.

2.   Put a large Dutch oven on a medium-high burner and add the oil. When the oil is hot, sear the beef on both sides until it's brown, about 6 to 8 minutes. Add the onion and garlic and cook 2 to 3 minutes, stirring, until lightly browned.

3.   Pour in the stock or water, cover with a lid, and put in the oven for 3 1/2 to 4 hours, until the meat is tender. (Check once or twice. If the roast looks dry during cooking, add another cupful of water or stock.)

4.   To serve, spoon a generous portion of meat into a split sandwich roll and top with some of the gravy. Cover and eat at once.

# The Chewiest Peanut Butter Cookie

This recipe is no secret, but if you haven't tried it, you may be surprised to find that it makes the peanut butter cookie of your dreams! It's chewy and dense, and bursting with peanut butter flavor. Use any brand of peanut butter, chunky or smooth, but you'll get a particularly good flavor and texture from natural peanut butter with salt but no added sugar.

*Makes 2 dozen*

1 cup peanut butter
1 cup sugar, plus more for dipping
1 egg

1. Preheat the oven to 350 degrees F. Cream together the peanut butter and sugar in a medium mixing bowl, then beat in the egg.

2. Shape the dough into 24 balls and divide them between 2 ungreased cookie sheets. Put a little sugar in a saucer or flat dish and dip a fork into it. Make a crisscross mark on top of each, to flatten the cookie.

3. Bake for 8 minutes, until just golden, and set. Don't overbake! As soon as the cookies smell as if they're done, they probably are.

# Salted Caramel Blondies

These little bites, with a delicate sprinkle of flaky salt on top, hit the perfect balance of sweet and salty, chewy and crisp, with the tangy hit of caramel in the back of your throat. They're quick, too—they take just moments to throw together and 15 minutes to bake. They disappear so fast, you may want two or three batches, but for best results, don't double the recipe—just make another batch on the heels of the first.

*Makes 64 tiny squares*

1/2 cup (1 stick) salted butter, melted
1 cup golden brown sugar
1 egg
1 teaspoon vanilla
1 cup all-purpose flour
1 scant teaspoon flaky salt, such as kosher Maldon sea salt or fleur de sel (or use a scant 1/4 teaspoon regular table salt)

1. Preheat the oven to 350 degrees F and grease an 8×8-inch metal baking pan.
2. Melt the butter in a medium saucepan or in a large microwavable bowl and beat in the sugar, egg, vanilla, and flour. Turn the mixture in to the prepared pan.
3. From a height of at least 8 inches, sprinkle the salt over the surface of the batter, being sure to get some onto the edges and corners. (Raising your hand high helps distribute the salt more evenly.)
4. Bake for 15 minutes, until lightly browned and just set in the center. Gooey is better than dry for these bars, so don't overbake. Cool before cutting into 64 pieces.

# ACKNOWLEDGMENTS

THIS BOOK WAS the idea of my terrific editor, Julie Ganz, and would never have happened without her support and cheerleading! Many thanks to Julie and all the excellent team at Skyhorse.

MY WIFE, SHARON Bowers, is always ready to drop everything and taste-test a batch of fudge. But more important, she's also always up for a trip to the supermarket, or yet another load of dishes. Honey, as always....

PARTICULAR THANKS AND love for my wonderful sons, Hugh and Pearse, who have evolved into surprisingly good little food critics. This one, as with everything, is for you.

# INDEX

# MY FAVORITE RECIPES

# METRIC AND IMPERIAL CONVERSIONS

(These conversions are rounded for convenience)

| Ingredient | Cups/Tablespoons/Teaspoons | Ounces | Grams/Milliliters |
|---|---|---|---|
| Butter | 1 cup=16 tablespoons= 2 sticks | 8 ounces | 230 grams |
| Cream cheese | 1 tablespoon | 0.5 ounce | 14.5 grams |
| Cheese, shredded | 1 cup | 4 ounces | 110 grams |
| Cornstarch | 1 tablespoon | 0.3 ounce | 8 grams |
| Flour, all-purpose | 1 cup/1 tablespoon | 4.5 ounces/0.3 ounce | 125 grams/8 grams |
| Flour, whole wheat | 1 cup | 4 ounces | 120 grams |
| Fruit, dried | 1 cup | 4 ounces | 120 grams |
| Fruits or veggies, chopped | 1 cup | 5 to 7 ounces | 145 to 200 grams |
| Fruits or veggies, pureed | 1 cup | 8.5 ounces | 245 grams |
| Honey, maple syrup, or corn syrup | 1 tablespoon | .75 ounce | 20 grams |
| Liquids: cream, milk, water, or juice | 1 cup | 8 fluid ounces | 240 ml |
| Oats | 1 cup | 5.5 ounces | 150 grams |
| Salt | 1 teaspoon | 0.2 ounces | 6 grams |
| Spices: cinnamon, cloves, ginger, or nutmeg (ground) | 1 teaspoon | 0.2 ounce | 5 ml |
| Sugar, brown, firmly packed | 1 cup | 7 ounces | 200 grams |
| Sugar, white | 1 cup/1 tablespoon | 7 ounces/0.5 ounce | 200 grams/12.5 grams |
| Vanilla extract | 1 teaspoon | 0.2 ounce | 4 grams |

# OVEN TEMPERATURES

| Fahrenheit | Celcius | Gas Mark |
|------------|---------|----------|
| 225° | 110° | ¼ |
| 250° | 120° | ½ |
| 275° | 140° | 1 |
| 300° | 150° | 2 |
| 325° | 160° | 3 |
| 350° | 180° | 4 |
| 375° | 190° | 5 |
| 400° | 200° | 6 |
| 425° | 220° | 7 |
| 450° | 230° | 8 |